Matching
Level One

Name

Date

■ Draw a line to the matching animal.

To parents

Guide your child to write his or her name and date in the box above. Do the exercise along with your child if he or she has difficulty.

■ Draw a line to the matching animal.

2

Matching
Level Two

Name

Date

■ Draw a line to the matching animal.

■ Draw a line to the matching animal.

Matching
Level Three

■ Draw a line to the matching animal.

Name

_____

Date

5

■ Draw a line to the matching animal.

6

Matching
Level Four

■ Draw a line to the matching animal.

Name

_____

Date

To parents
The activity is now more difficult because the animal is partly hidden. Guide your child to look at the features that are visible.

7

■ Draw a line to the matching animal.

Matching
Level Five

■ Draw a line to the matching animal.

Name

Date

To parents
If your child has difficulty, ask him or her to try to identify the animal hidden behind the plant.

■ Draw a line to the matching animal.

10

Matching
Level Six

■ Draw a line to the matching animal.

Name

Date

To parents

The number of answer choices has increased. If your child has difficulty, help him or her eliminate answer choices one by one.

■ Draw a line to the matching animal.

Matching
Level Seven

Name

_____

Date

■ Draw a line to the matching animal.

■ Draw a line to the matching animal.

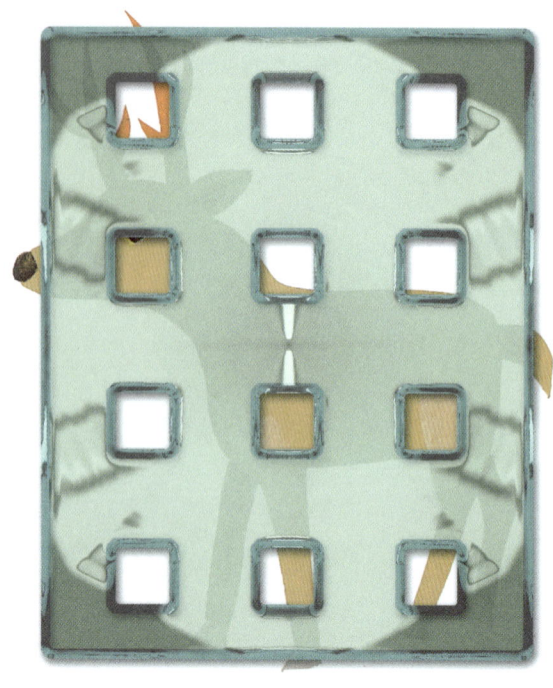

14

Matching
Level Eight

■ Draw a line to the matching animal.

Name

Date

To parents

If your child has difficulty, ask him or her to identify the animal shown on the left first, before looking for the matching picture.

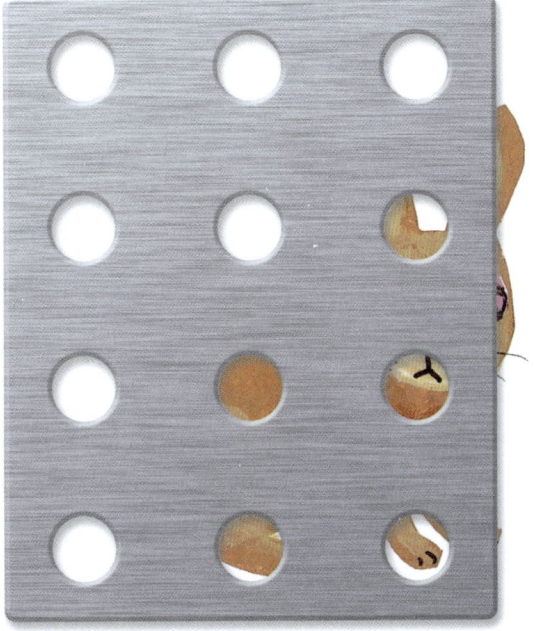

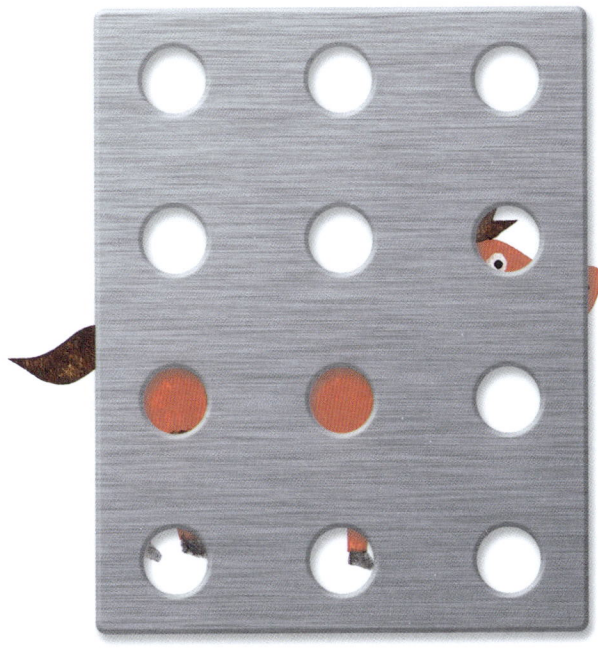

■ Draw a line to the matching animal.

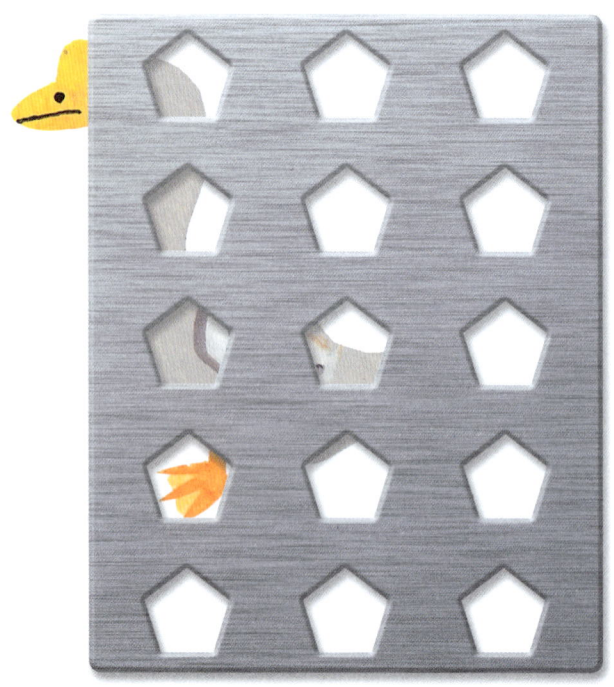

16

Matching
Level Nine

■ Draw a line to the matching animal.

Name

Date

To parents
The number of answer choices has increased. Encourage your child to look carefully at each one.

17

■ Draw a line to the matching animal.

Matching
Level One

■ Draw a line to the matching picture.

Name

Date

To parents
Help your child look carefully at the position or pose shown in each picture.

■ Draw a line to the matching picture.

20

 **Matching**
Level Two

Name

Date

■ Draw a line to the picture that shows the same position.

To parents
Now the pictures on the right show a different person. Encourage your child to match the same position or pose.

■ Draw a line to the picture that shows the same position.

22

Matching
Level Three

Name

Date

To parents
If your child has difficulty, work together to point out small details in the pictures such as whether an animal's mouth is open or closed.

■ Draw a line to the picture that shows the same position.

Matching Mirror Images

Level One

Name

Date

■ Draw a line to the mirror image.

To parents

For a hands-on example, place a small mirror at a right angle with one of the pictures on this page. Have your child compare the picture with the mirror image.

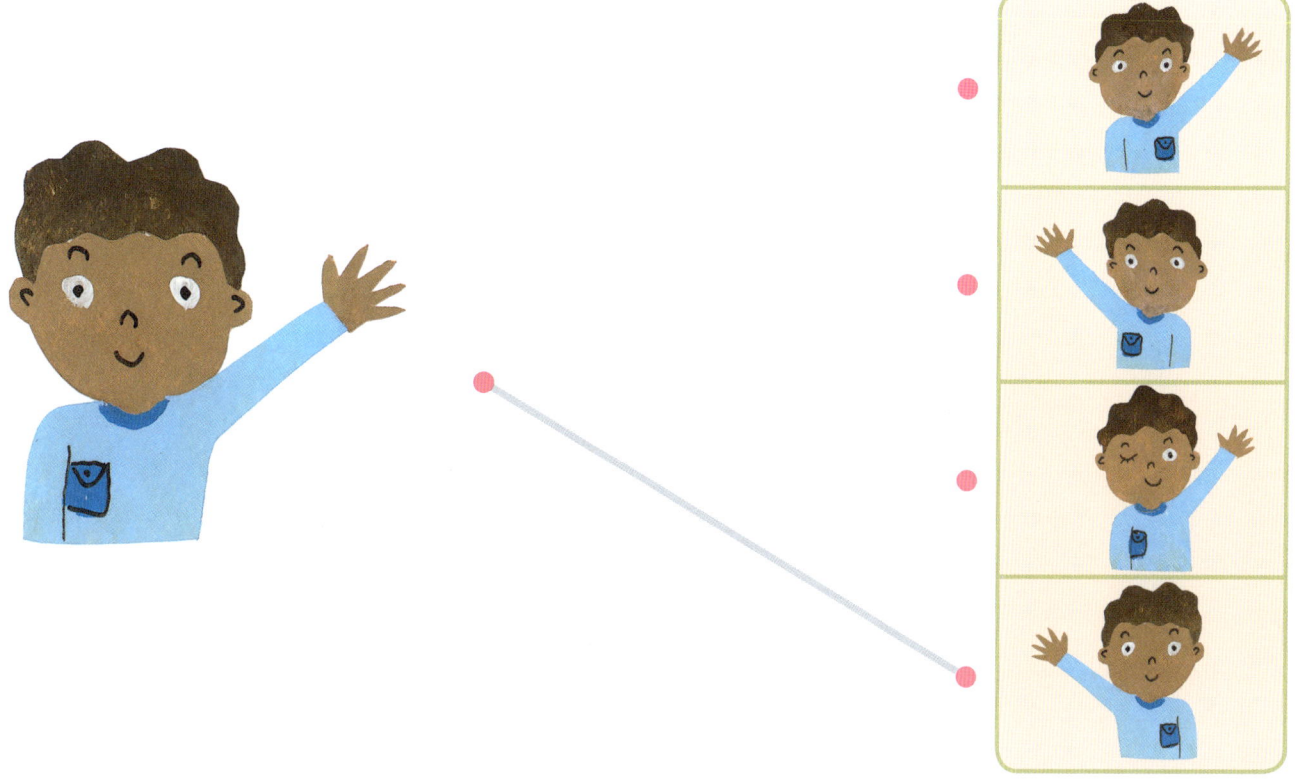

25

■ Draw a line to the mirror image.

Matching Mirror Images

Level Two

Name

Date

■ Draw a line to the mirror image of the position.

27

■ Draw a line to the mirror image of the position.

28

Matching Mirror Images

Level Three

■ Draw a line to the mirror image of
  the position.

To parents

The number of answer choices has increased. Encourage your
child to look carefully at each one.

Name

Date

29

■ Draw a line to the mirror image of the position.

30

16 Matching Quantity
Level One

Name

Date

■ Draw a line to the picture that has same number of objects.

To parents
If your child has difficulty, count the objects in the pictures together.

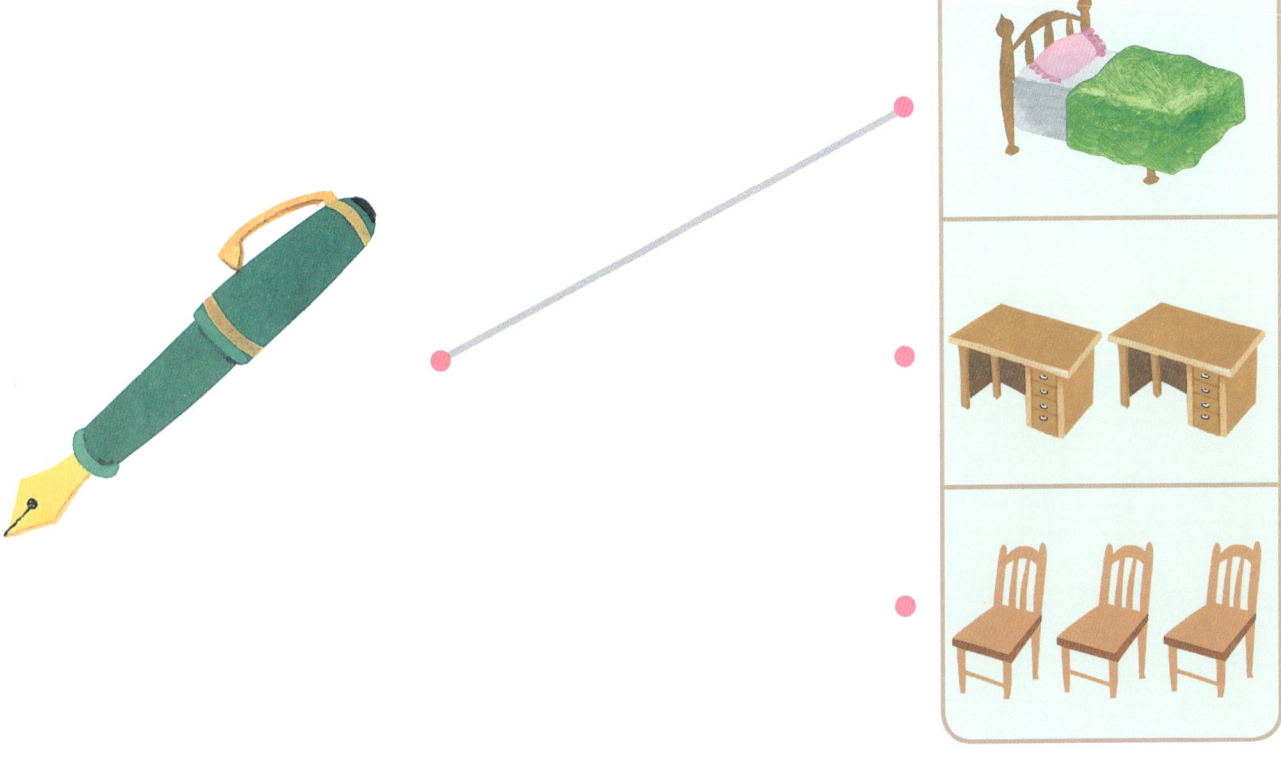

■ Draw a line to the picture that has same number of objects.

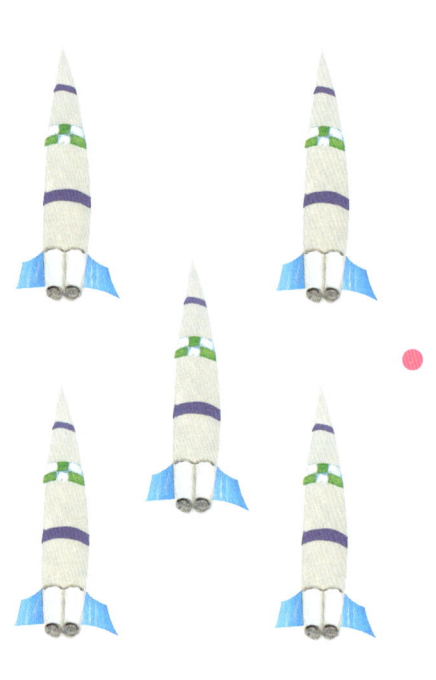

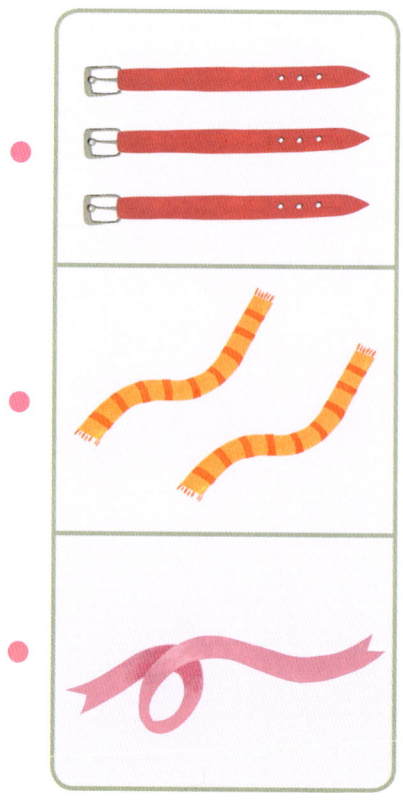

32

Matching Quantity
Level Two

■ Draw a line to the picture that has same number of objects.

To parents

The number of answer choices in the right column has increased. Encourage your child to look carefully at each one.

Name

Date

■ Draw a line to the picture that has same number of objects.

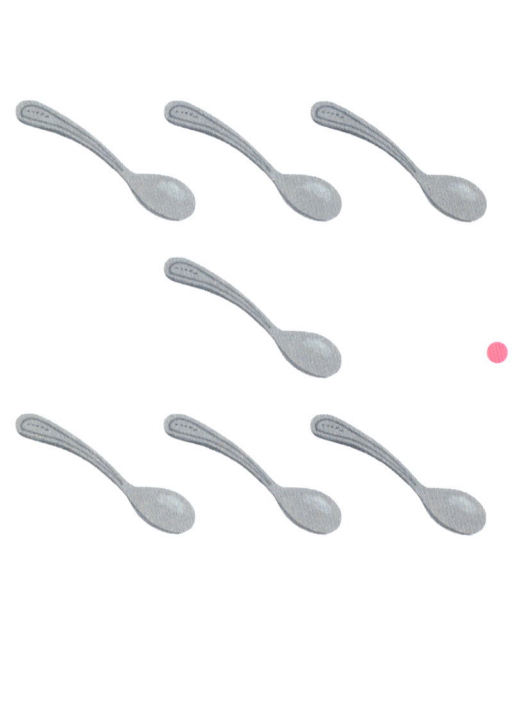

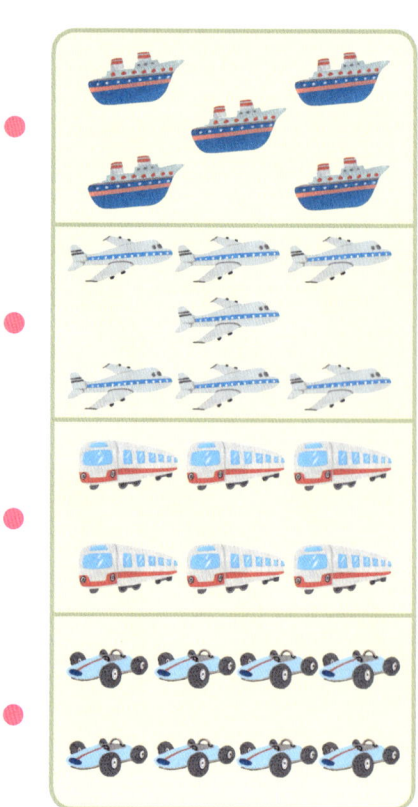

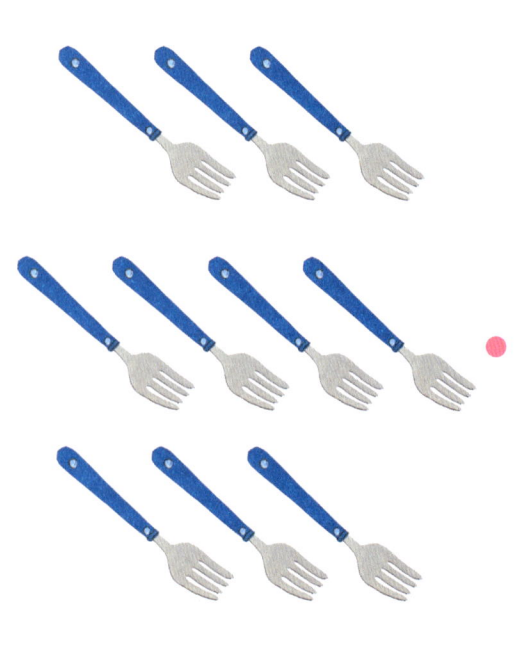

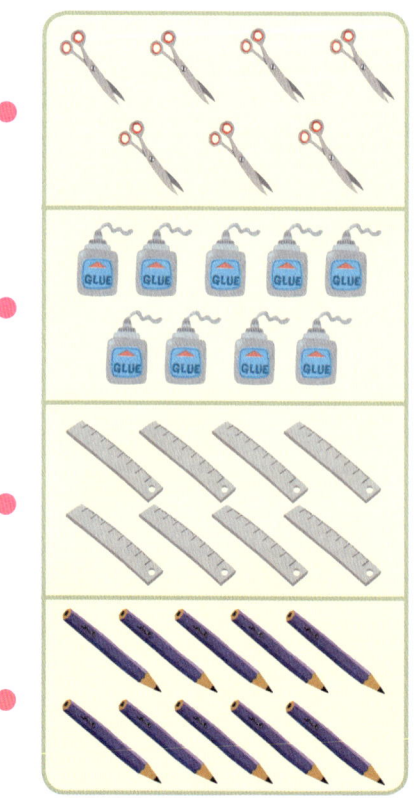

34

Matching Quantity
Level Three

Name

Date

■ Draw a line between the pictures that have the same number of objects.

To parents
If your child has difficulty, guide him or her to match each picture on the left with one on the right.

■ Draw a line between the pictures that have the same number of objects.

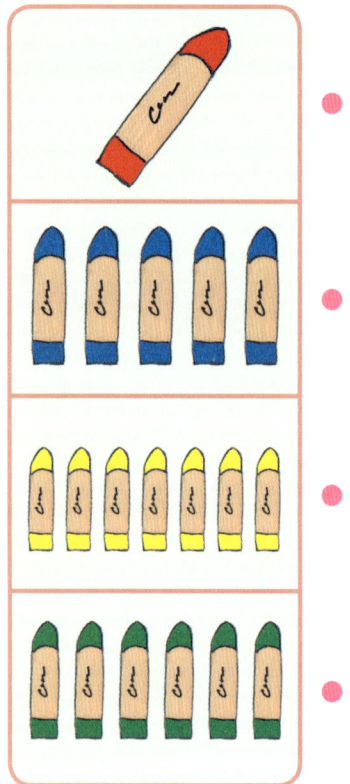

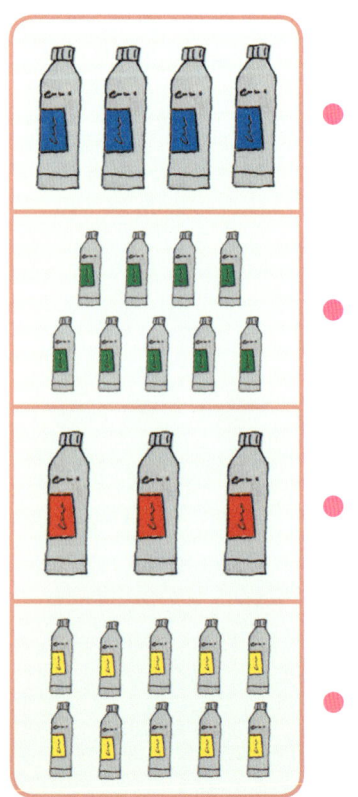

Matching Quantity
Level Four

Name

Date

■ Draw a line to the matching picture.

To parents

If your child has difficulty, ask him or her to describe how much water is in each glass.

■ Draw a line to the matching picture.

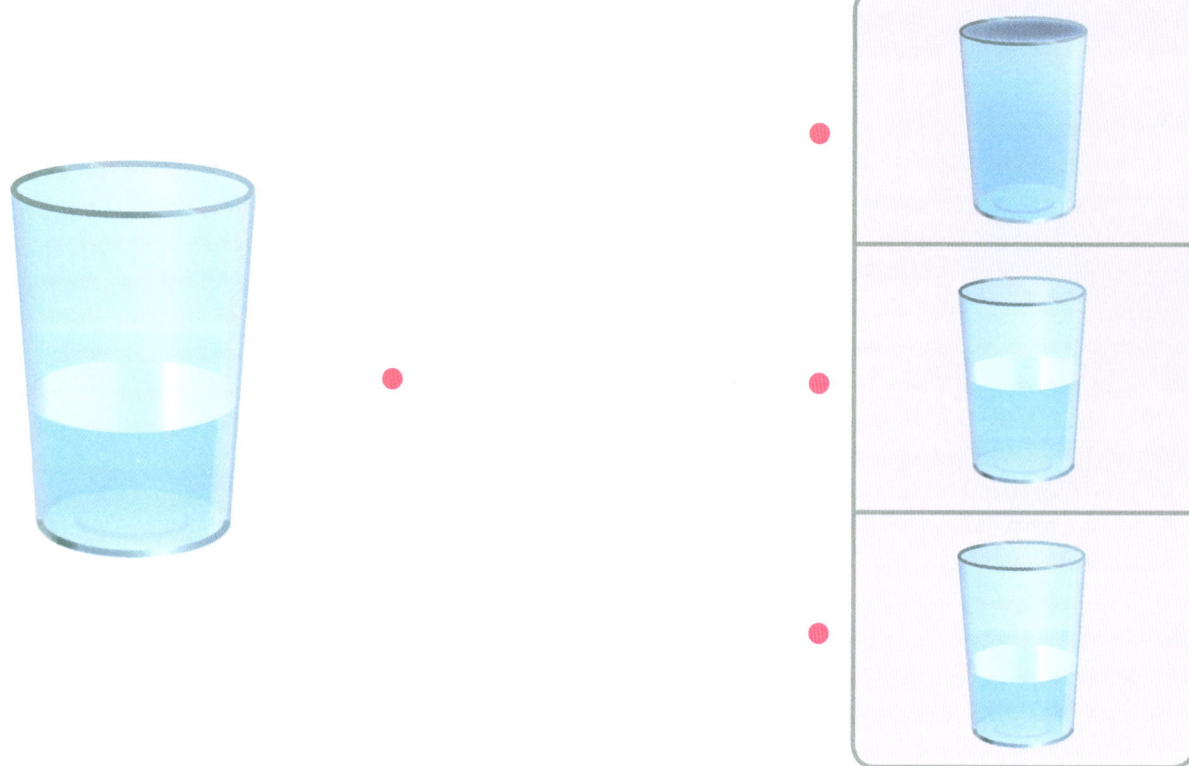

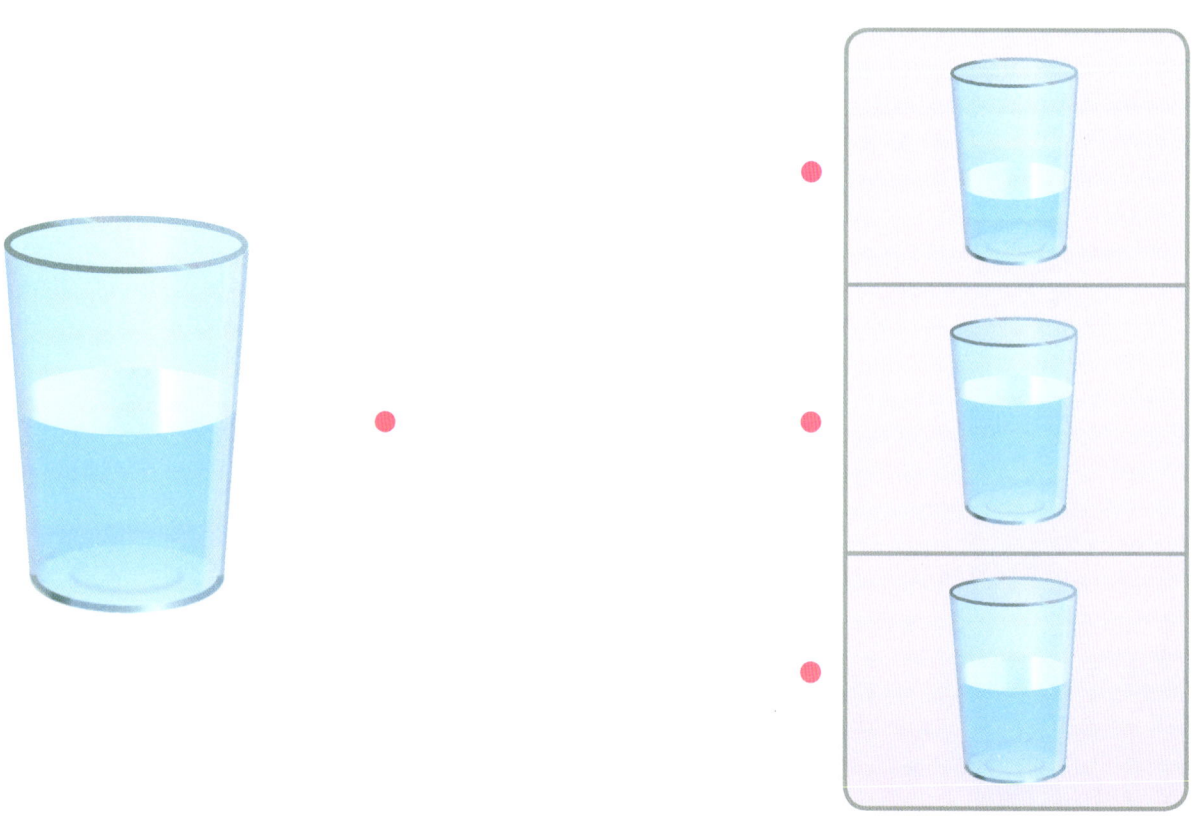

Matching Quantity
Level Five

■ Draw a line to the matching picture.

Name

Date

To parents

There are now four answer choices. If your child has difficulty, encourage him or her to look at each glass carefully.

■ Draw a line to the matching picture.

Matching Quantity
Level Six

■ Draw a line between the matching pictures.

To parents

If your child has difficulty, guide him or her to match each picture on the left with one on the right.

41

■ Draw a line between the matching pictures.

42

22 Finding the Missing Object

Level One

Name

Date

■ Draw a line to the object that goes best with the picture.

To parents
If your child has difficulty, ask him or her to identify each person's job.

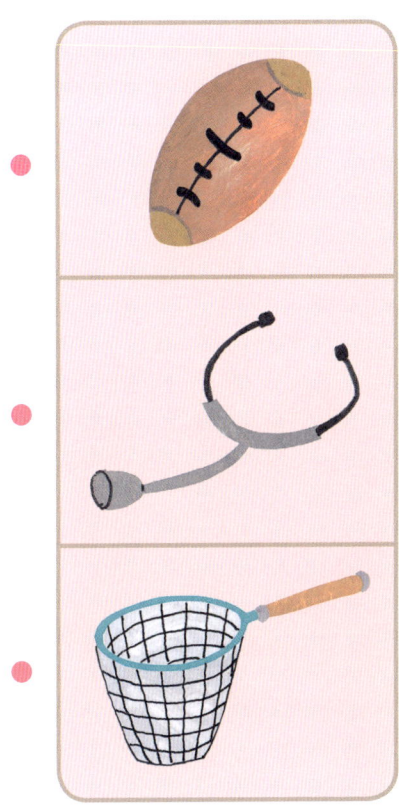

■ Draw a line to the object that goes best with the picture.

Finding the Missing Object

Level Two

Name

Date

■ Draw a line to the object that goes best with the picture.

To parents
If your child has difficulty, ask him or her what object each person is holding.

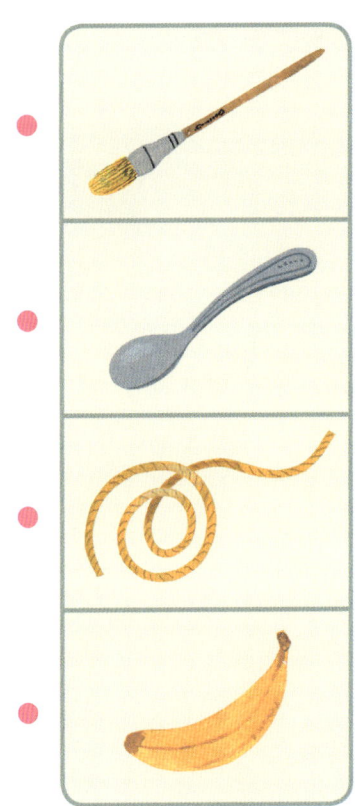

45

■ Draw a line to the object that goes best with the picture.

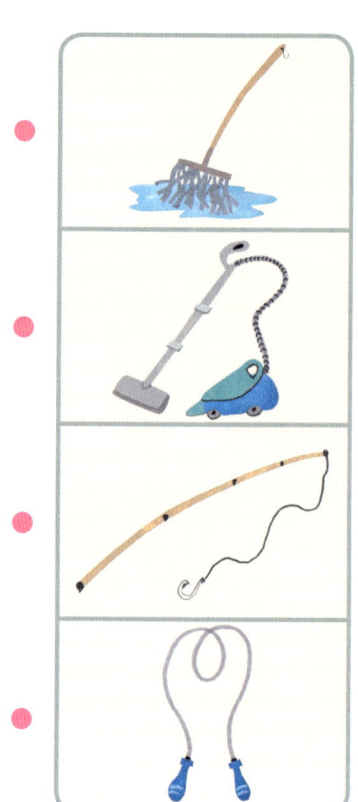

Finding the Missing Object

Level Three

Name

Date

■ Draw a line to the missing object.

To parents
Encourage your child to look carefully at all the colors in the box to find the missing color.

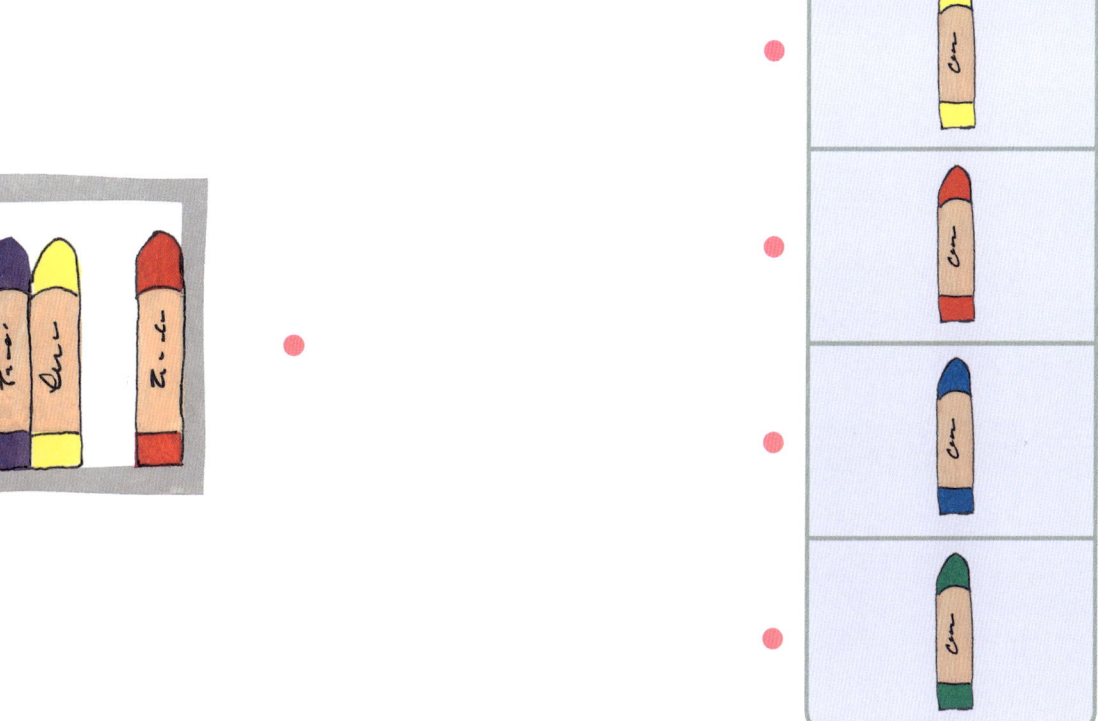

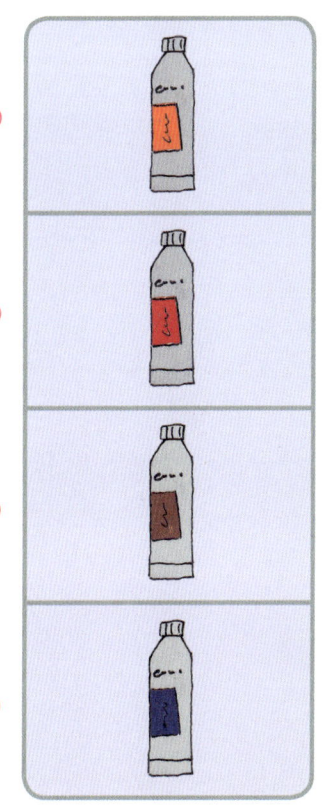

■ Draw a line to the missing object.

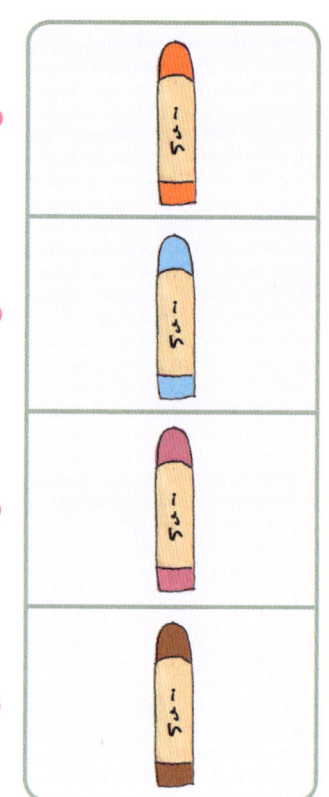

48

Differentiation
Level One

Name

Date

To parents
All five objects are in the same general category. Help your child find the two that are the most similar.

■ Write a check mark (✓) above the two pictures that are the most similar.

( )   ( )   ( )

( )   ( )

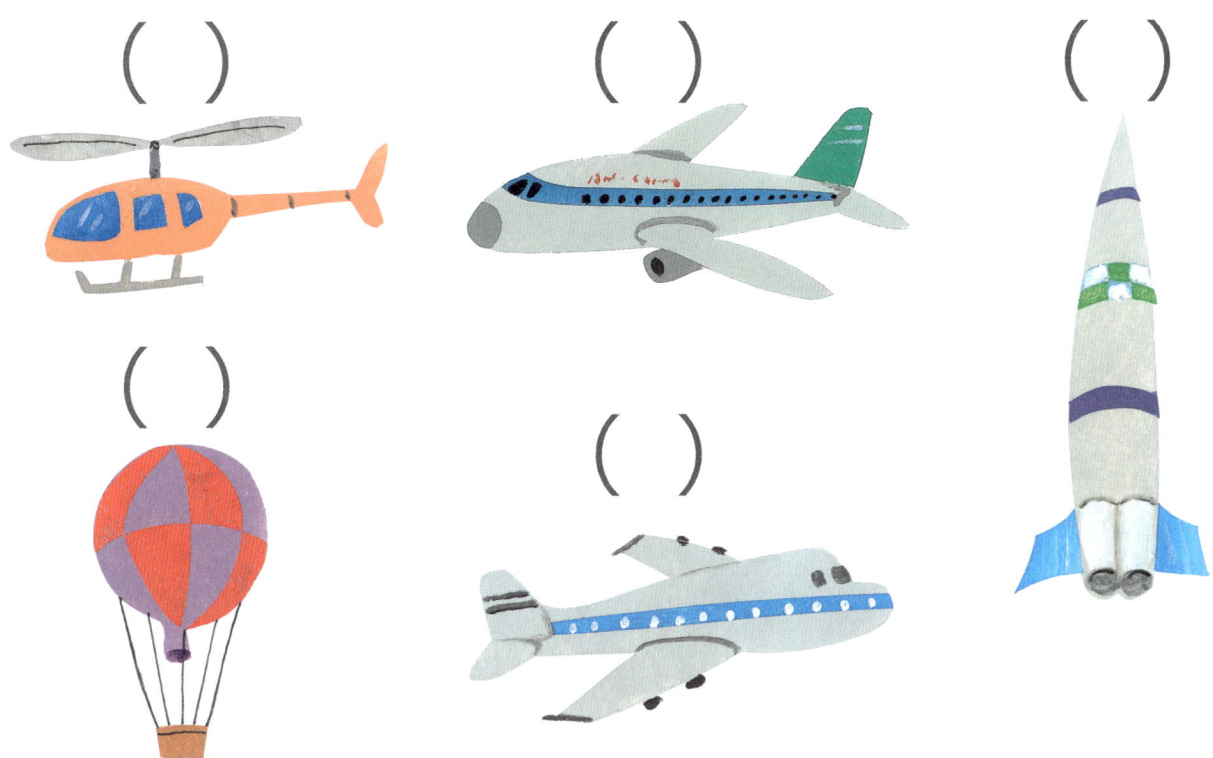

( )   ( )   ( )

( )   ( )

■ Write a check mark (✓) above the two pictures that are the most similar.

50

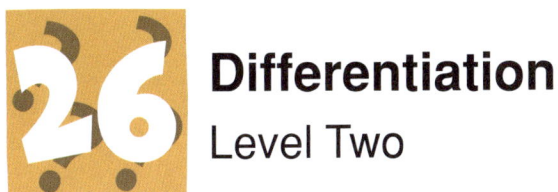

Differentiation
Level Two

Name

Date

■ Write a check mark (✓) above the three animals that are the most similar.

To parents
If your child has difficulty, help him or her look for a group of exactly three animals that do something similar.

( )

( )

( )

( )

( )

( )

( )

( )

( )

( )

51

■ Write a check mark (✓) above the three animals that are the most similar.

Differentiation
Level Three

Name

Date

To parents
If your child has difficulty, ask him or her to briefly describe each object to find similar characteristics.

■ Write a check mark (✓) above the three pictures that are the most similar.

(　　)   (　　)   (　　)   (　　)

(　　)   (　　)   (　　)   (　　)

(　　)   (　　)   (　　)   (　　)

53

■ Write a check mark (✓) above the three animals that are doing something similar.

Matching Pairs
Level One

Name

Date

■ Write a check mark (✓) under the picture without a match.

To parents

If your child has difficulty, show him or her how to eliminate answer choices by crossing off matching pairs.

( ) ( ) ( ) ( )

( ) ( ) ( ) ( )

( ) ( ) ( )

■ Write a check mark (✓) under the picture without a match.

( )　　　　( )　　　　( )　　　　( )

( )　　　　( )　　　　( )　　　　( )

( )　　　　( )　　　　( )

56

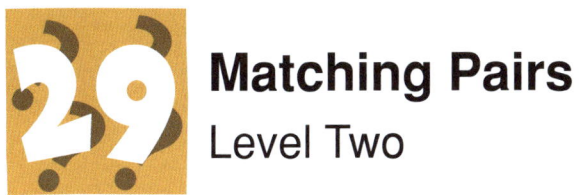

Matching Pairs
Level Two

Name

Date

■ Write a check mark (✓) under the picture without a match.

To parents
If your child has difficulty, guide him or her to look at each picture one by one and check if it has a match.

( )   ( )   ( )

( )   ( )   ( )   ( )

( )   ( )   ( )

( )   ( )   ( )

■ Write a check mark (✓) under the picture without a match.

58

30

Matching Pairs

Level Three

Name

Date

To parents

Encourage your child to look carefully at each animal's pose or position.

■ Write a check mark (✓) under the picture without a match.

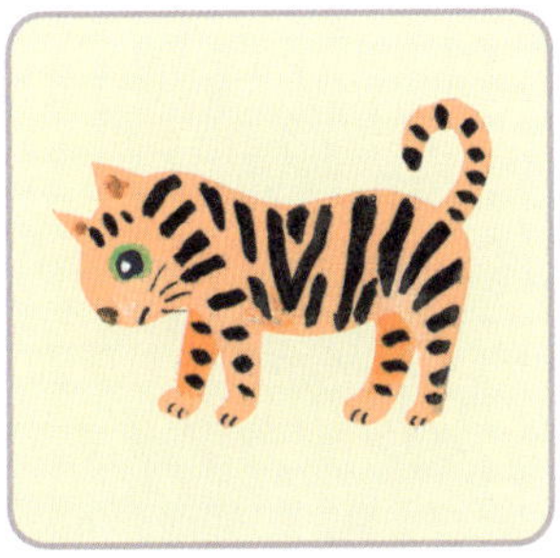

( )

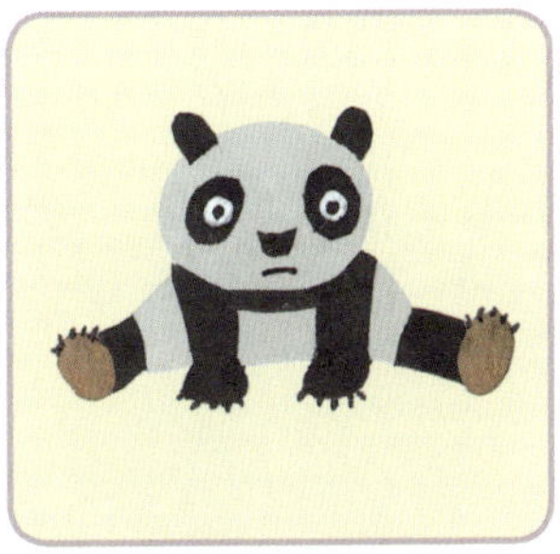

( )

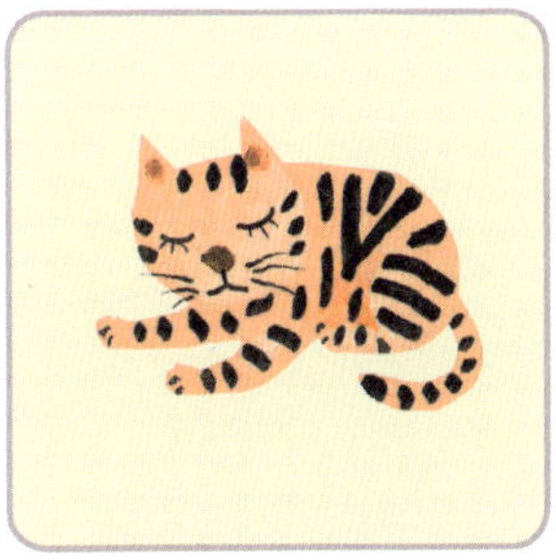

( )

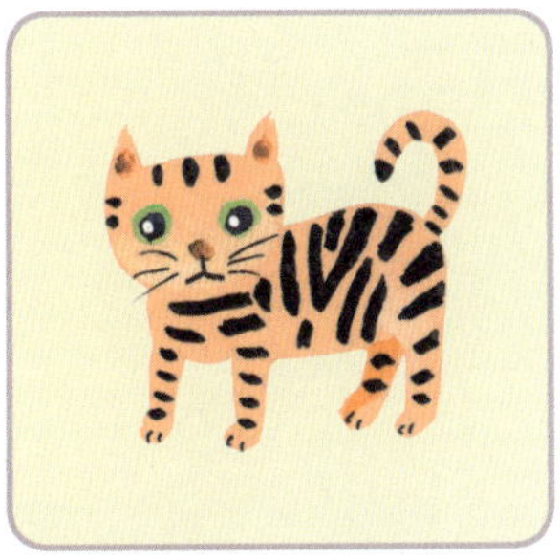

( )

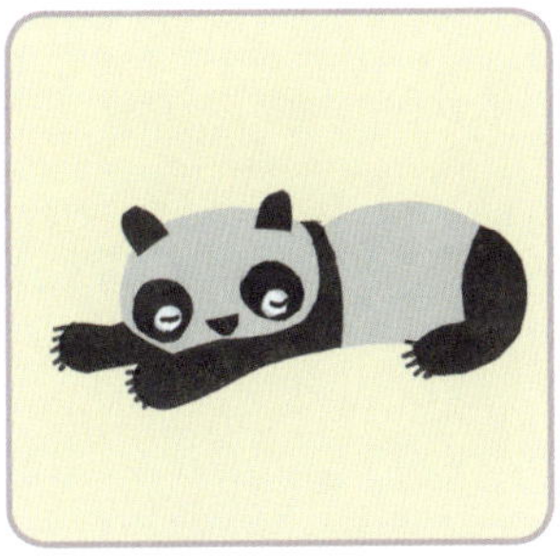

( )

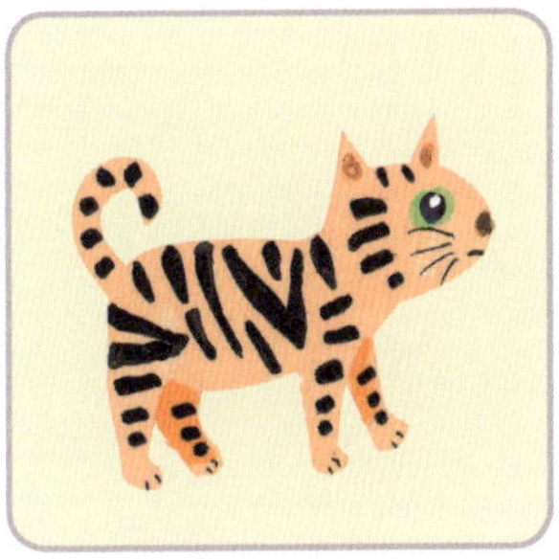

( )

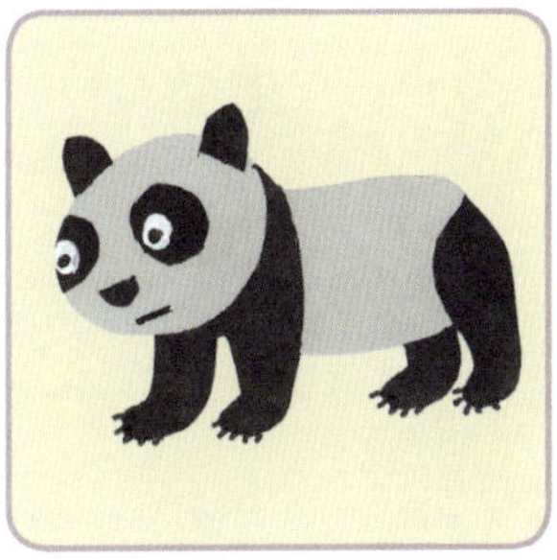

( )

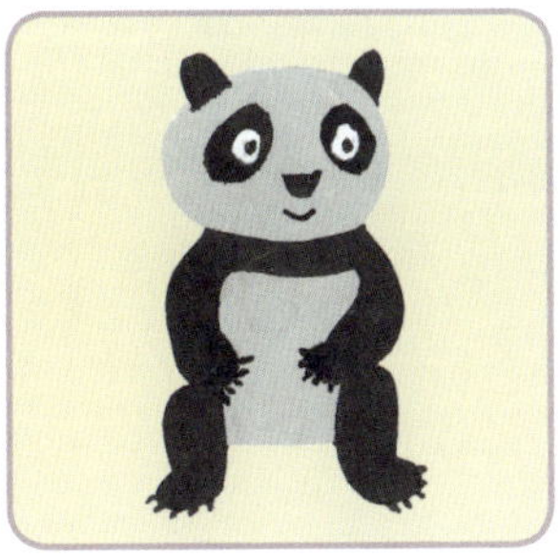

( )

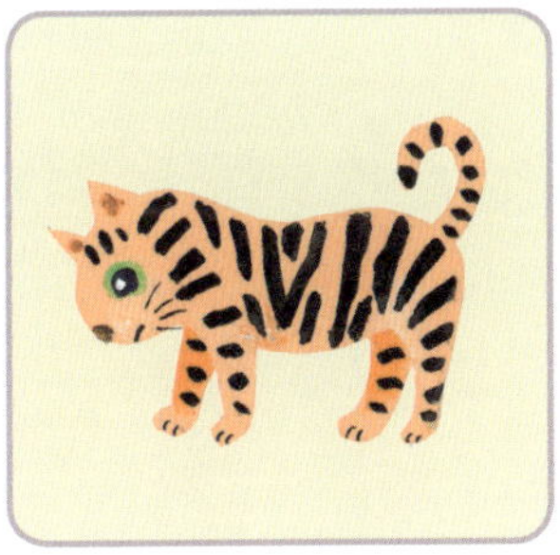

( )

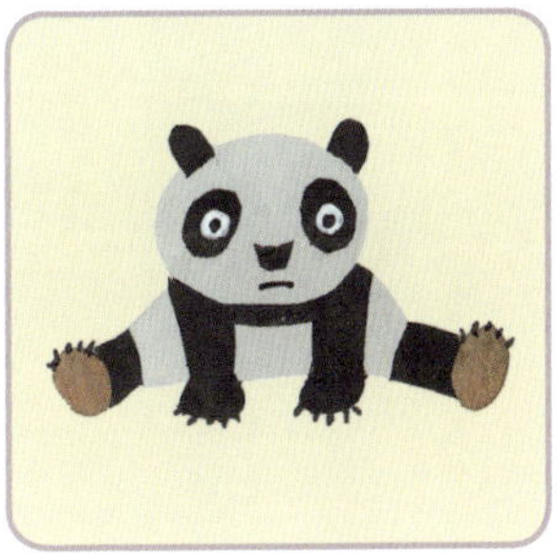

( )

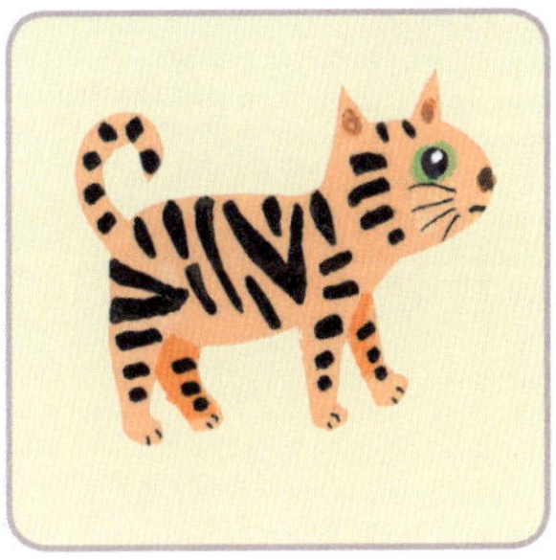

( )

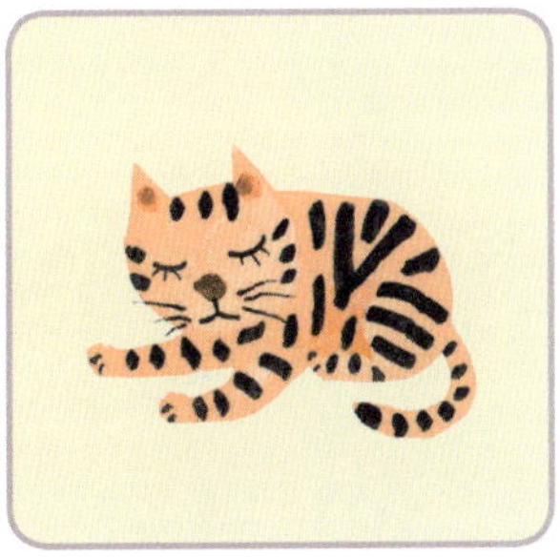

( )

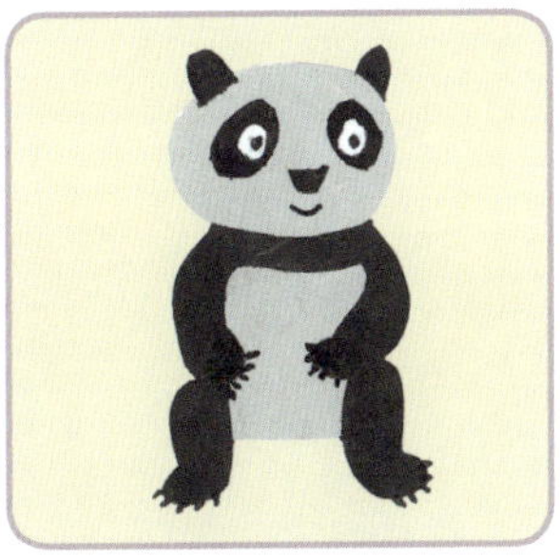

( )

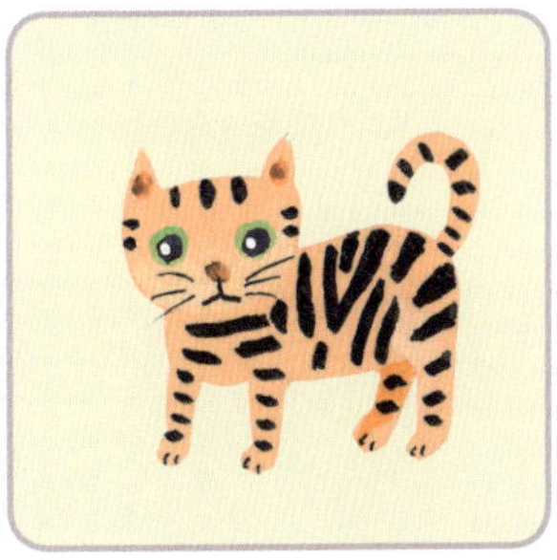

( )

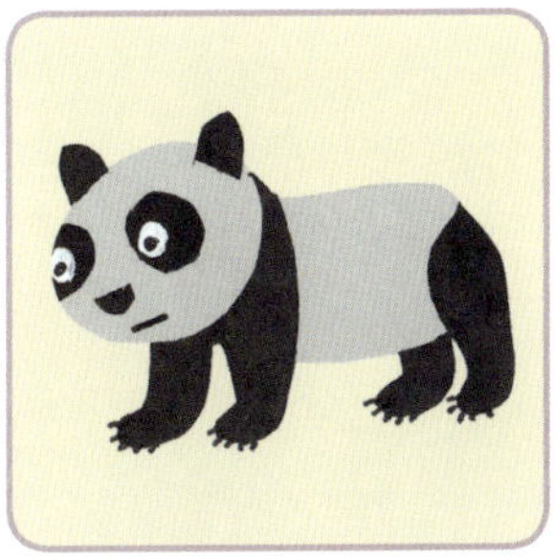

( )

■ Write a check mark (✓) under the picture without a match.

(　)　　　　(　)　　　　(　)

(　)　　　　(　)　　　　(　)　　　　(　)

(　)　　　　(　)　　　　(　)　　　　(　)

(　)　　　　(　)　　　　(　)　　　　(　)

31 Identifying Objects
Level One

Name

Date

To parents

Point to an object shown in the instructions. Guide your child to find the same object in the picture below.

- Find and circle the following objects in the picture below: (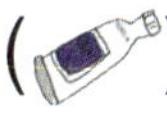) (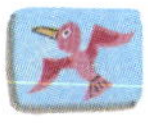) (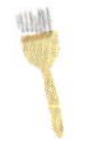)

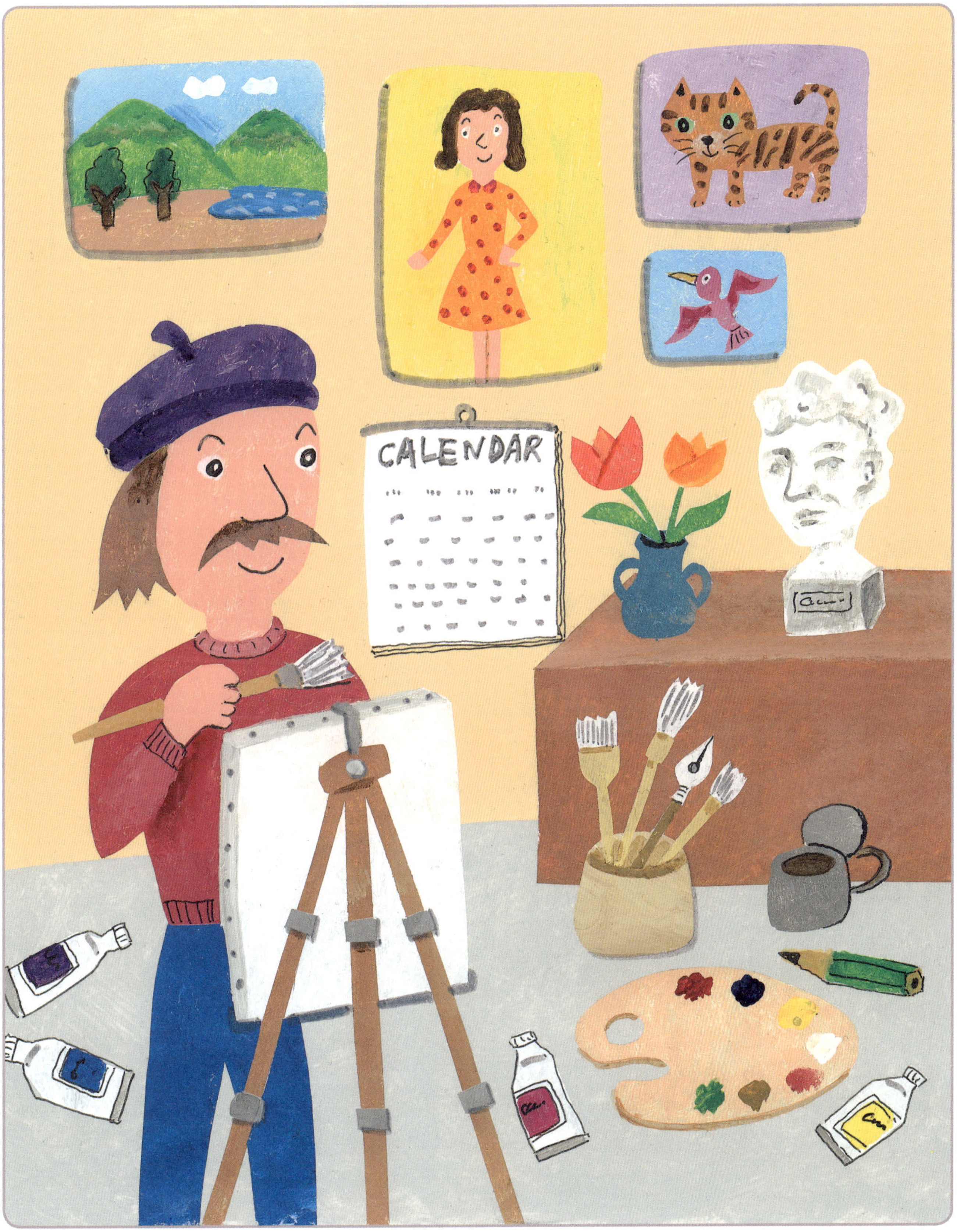

■ Find and circle the following objects in the picture below:

() ( ) ( )

Identifying Objects
Level Two

Name

Date

■ Find and circle the following animals in the picture below: ( ) ( ) ( ) ( )

To parents

If your child enjoys looking at the picture, encourage him or her to identify other objects in the scene.

■ Find and circle the following fish in the picture below:

33 Identifying Objects

Level Three

Name

Date

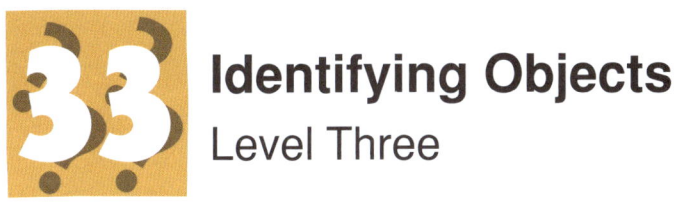

To parents

The number of different objects to find and circle has increased. Encourage your child to look for all five objects.

■ Find and circle the following objects in the picture below: (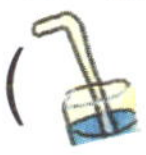) (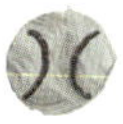) (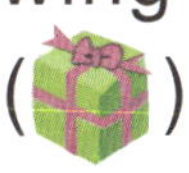) (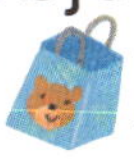) (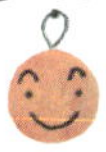)

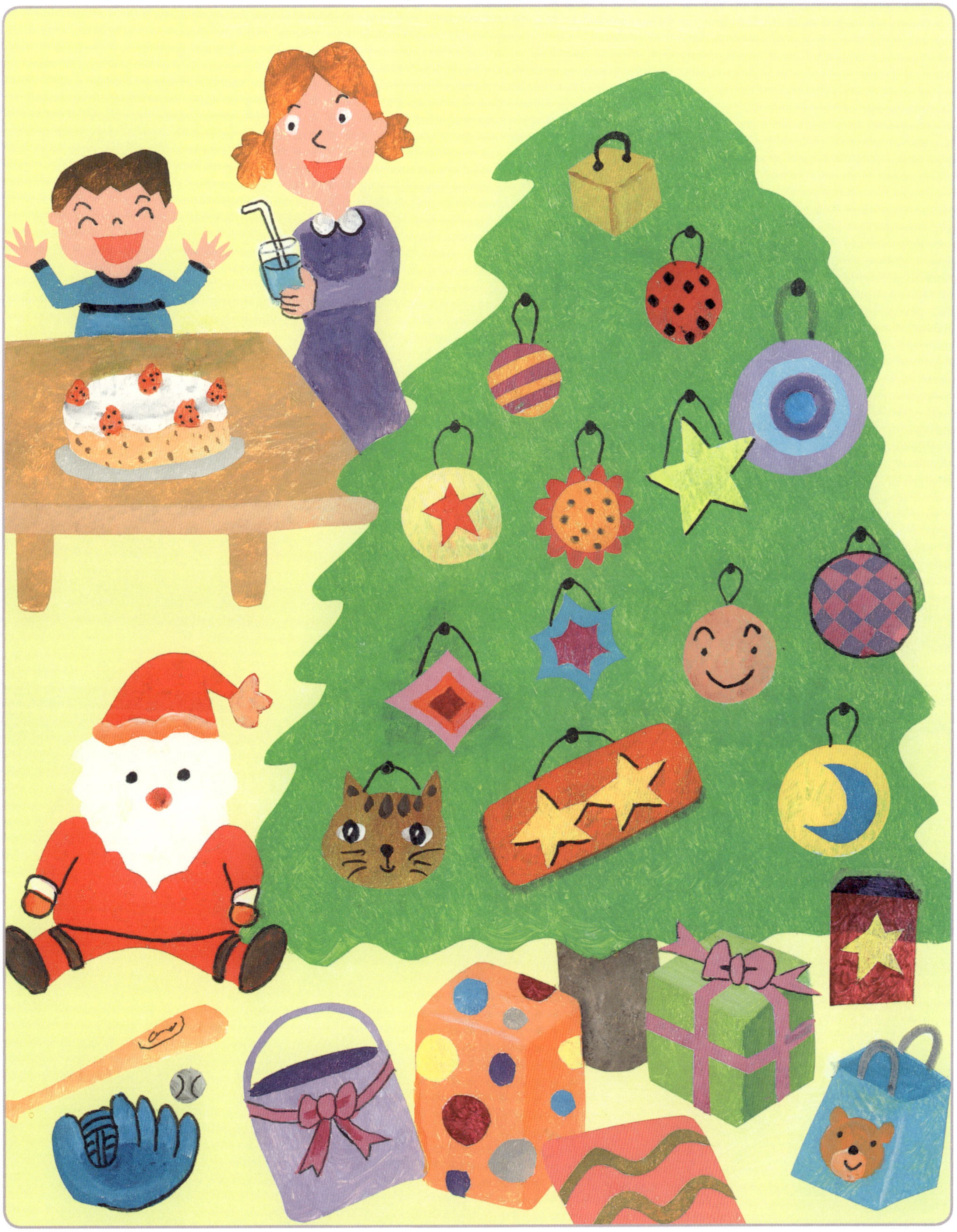

■ Find and circle the following objects in the picture below:

34 Identifying Objects
Level Four

Name

Date

To parents
Encourage your child to look carefully at the objects in the instructions first.

■ Find and circle the following shells in the picture below: (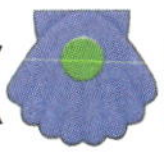) (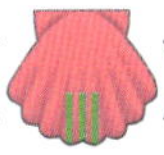)

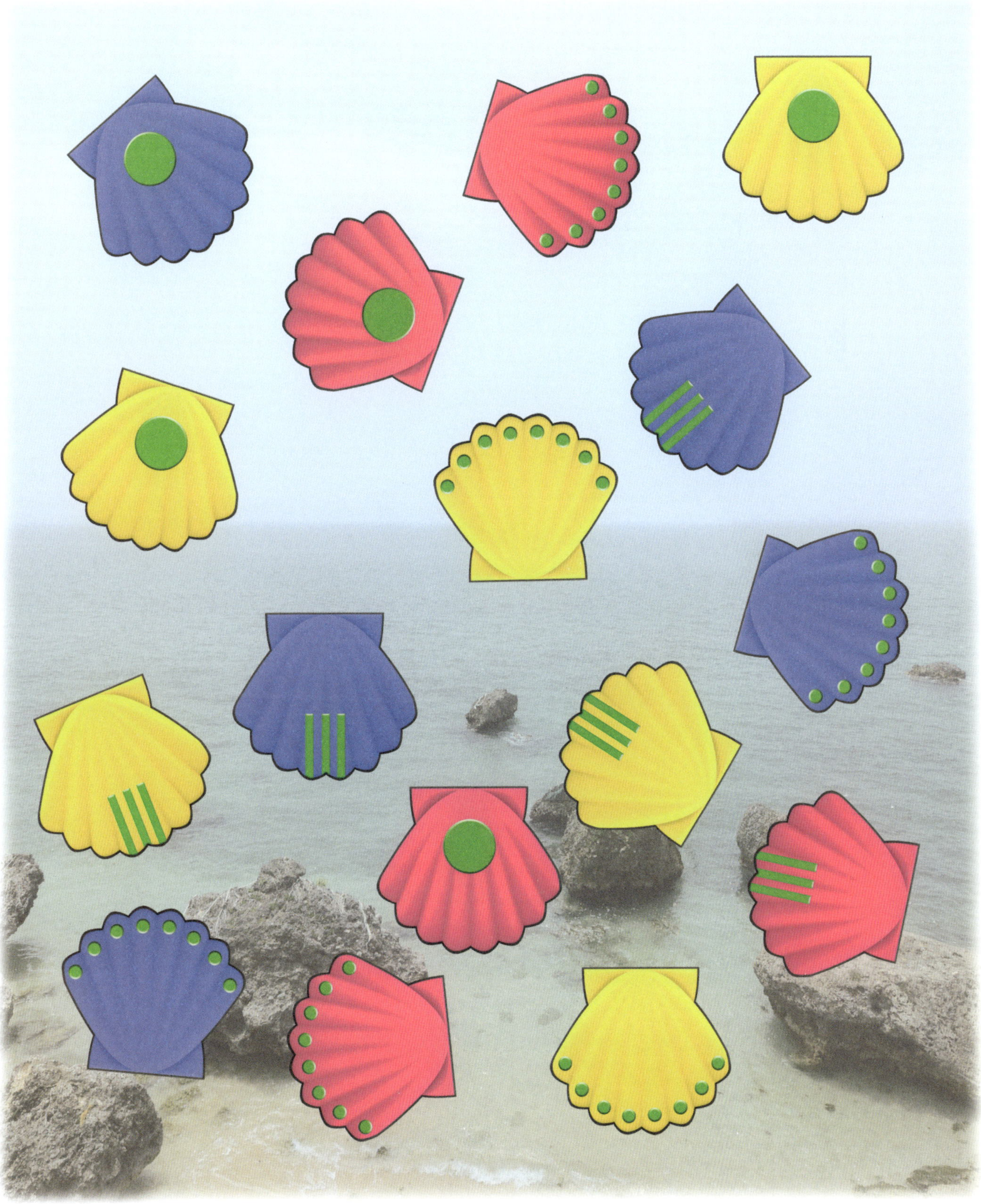

■Find and circle the following can and bottle in the picture below:

(🥫) (🍾)

35

Identifying Objects
Level Five

Name

Date

To parents

The number of objects in the picture has increased. Guide your child to find the same objects shown in the instructions.

■ Find and circle the following blocks in the picture below:

■ Find and circle the following pendants in the picture below:

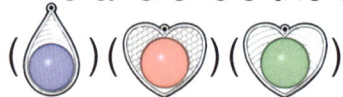

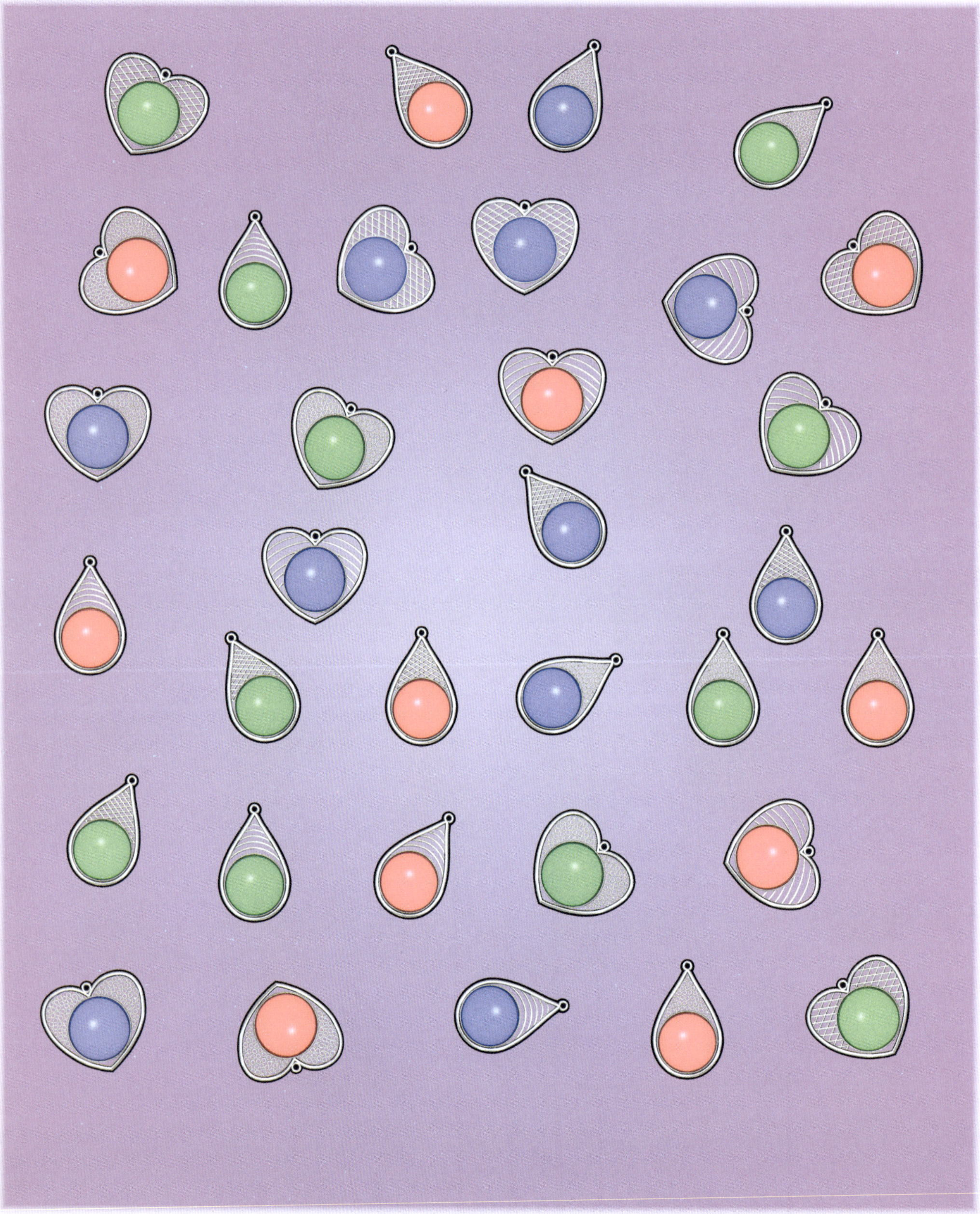

36

Identifying Objects
Level Six

Name

Date

To parents

If your child has difficulty, encourage him or her to look at each object one by one and check if it is one of the objects in the instructions.

■ Find and circle the following cups in the picture below:

To parents
This is the last exercise of this workbook. Please praise your child for the effort it took to complete this workbook.

■ Find and circle the following masks in the picture below:

() ( ) () ( )

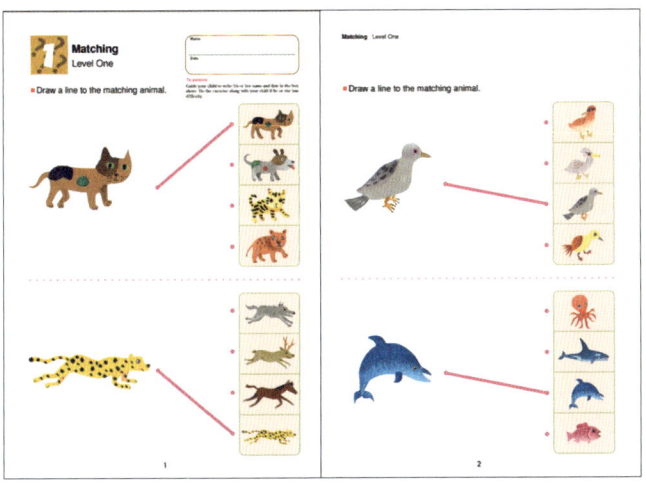

pages 1 and 2

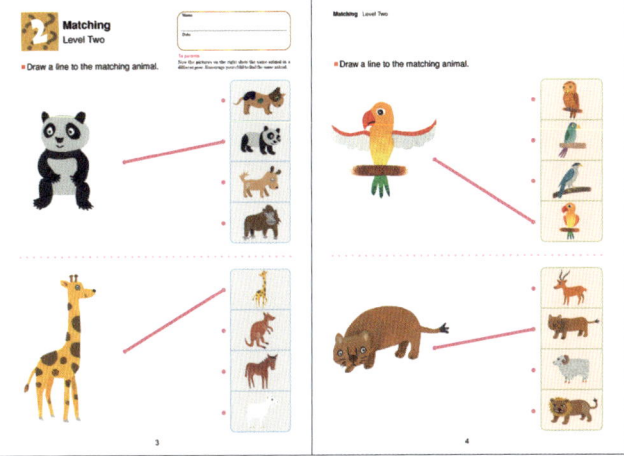

pages 3 and 4

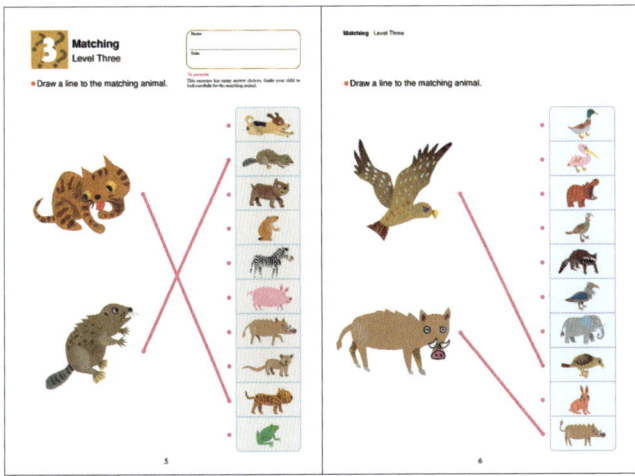

pages 5 and 6

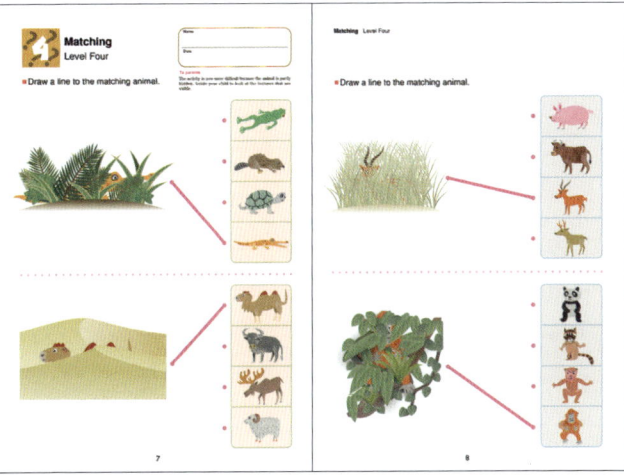

pages 7 and 8

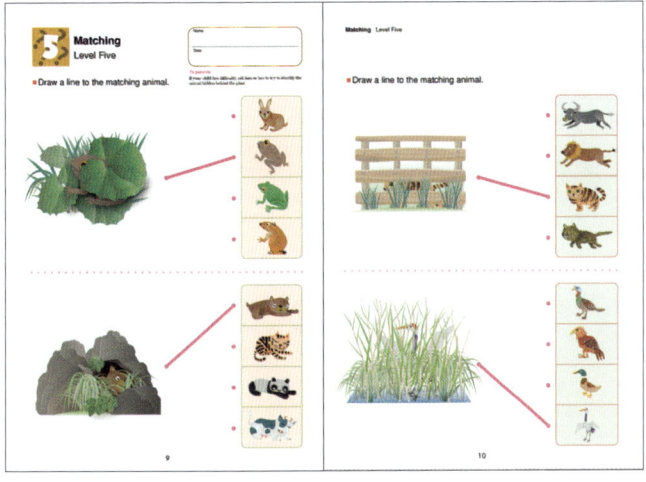

pages 9 and 10

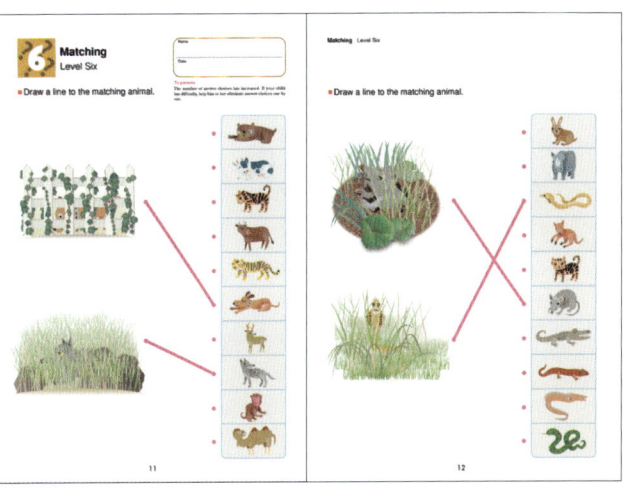

pages 11 and 12

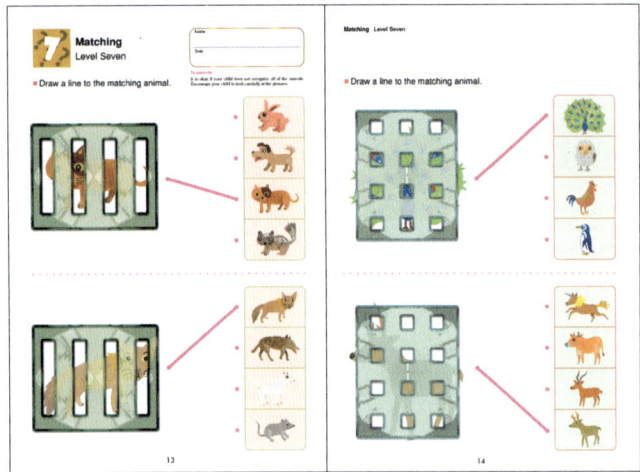

pages 13 and 14

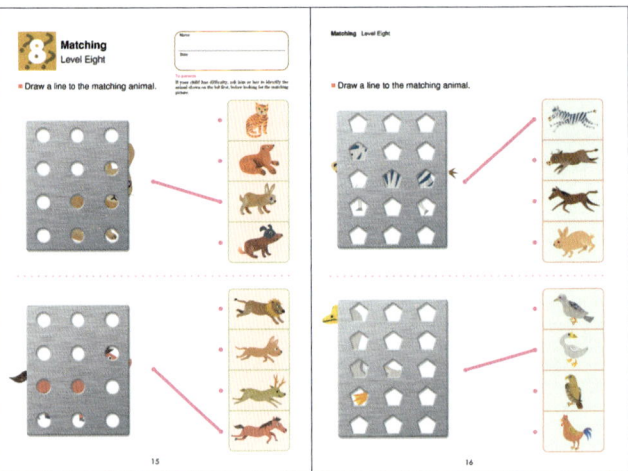

pages 15 and 16

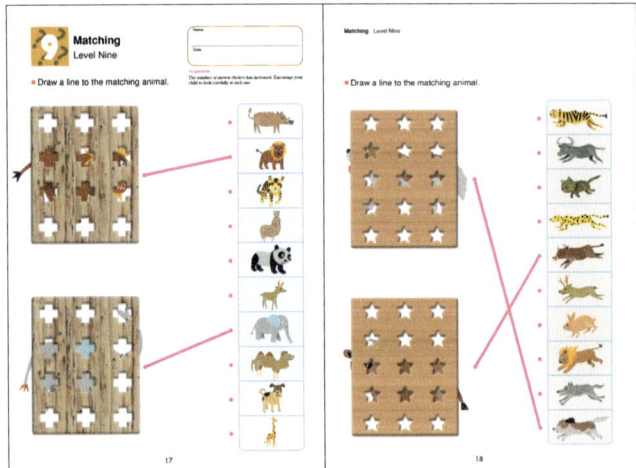

pages 17 and 18

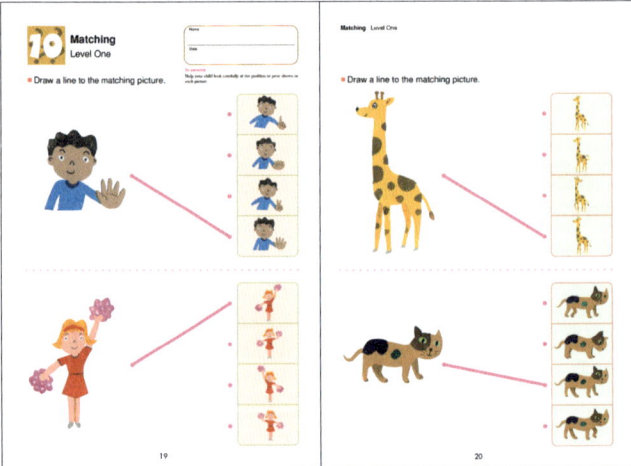

pages 19 and 20

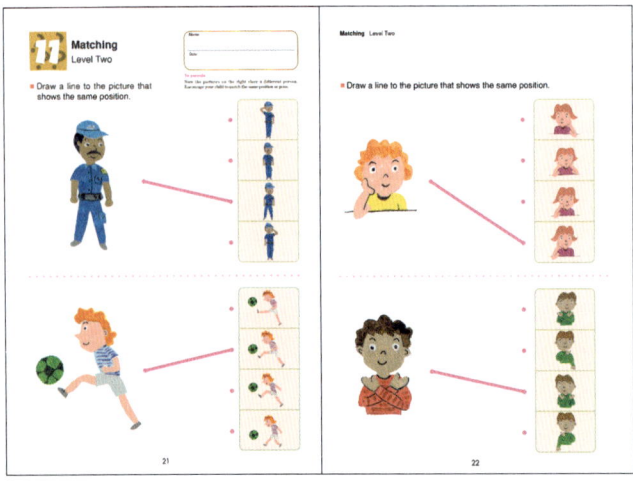

pages 21 and 22

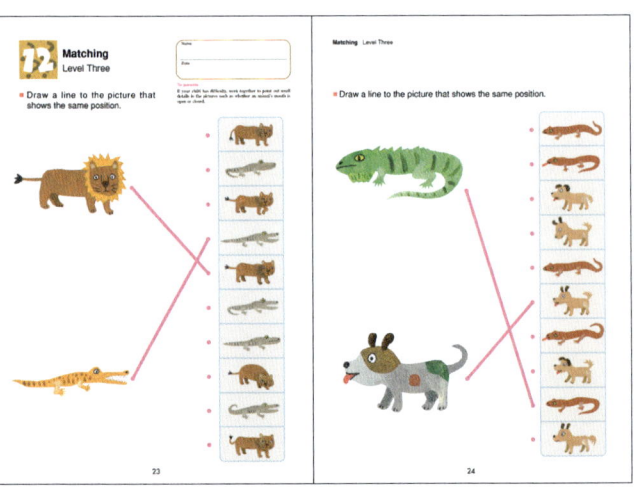

pages 23 and 24

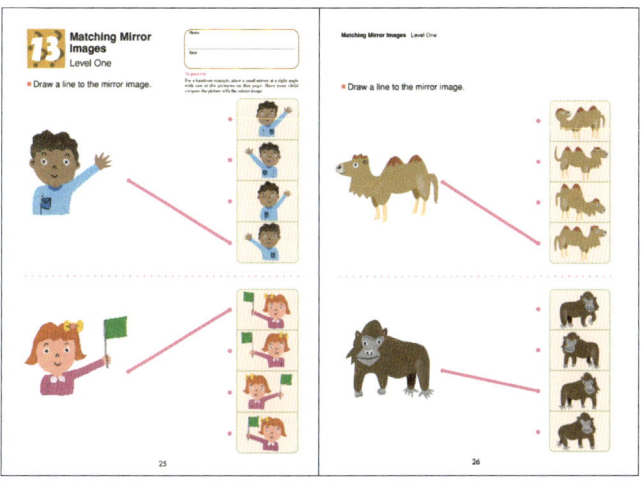

pages 25 and 26

pages 27 and 28

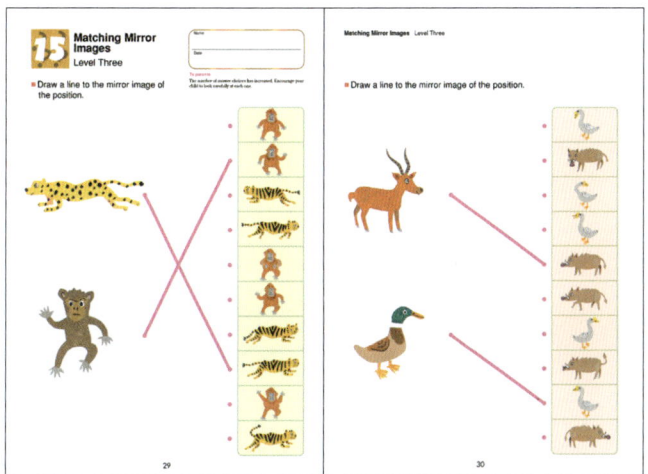

pages 29 and 30

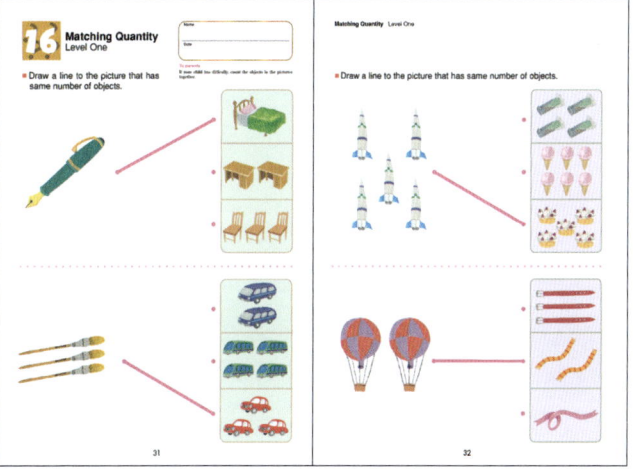

pages 31 and 32

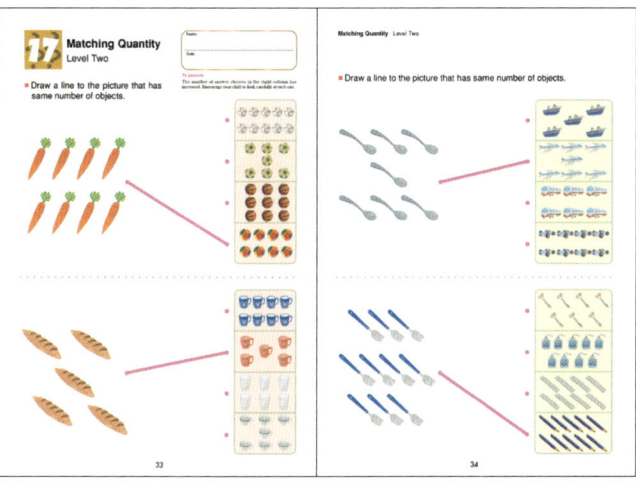

pages 33 and 34

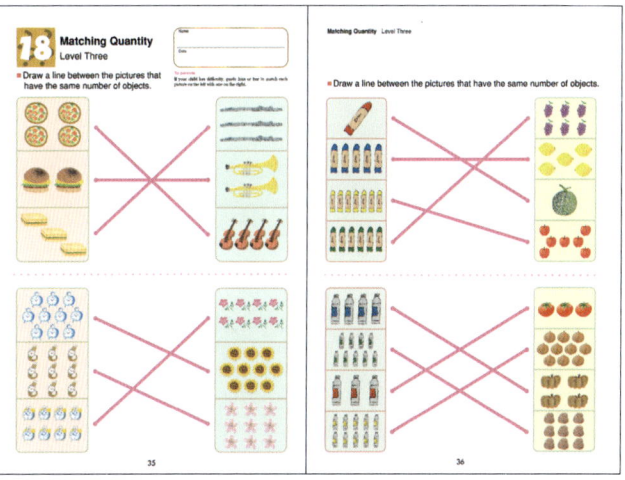

pages 35 and 36

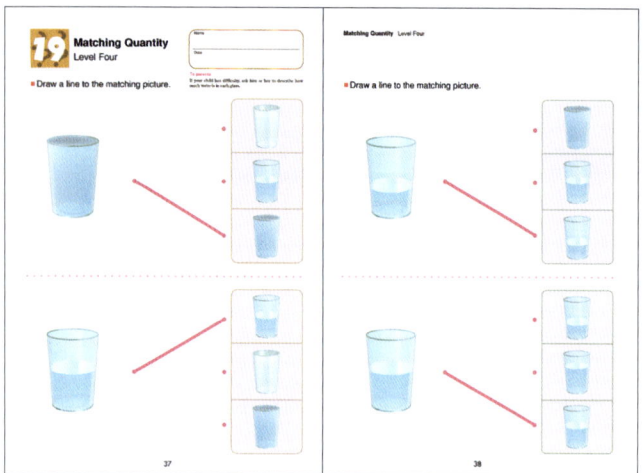

pages 37 and 38

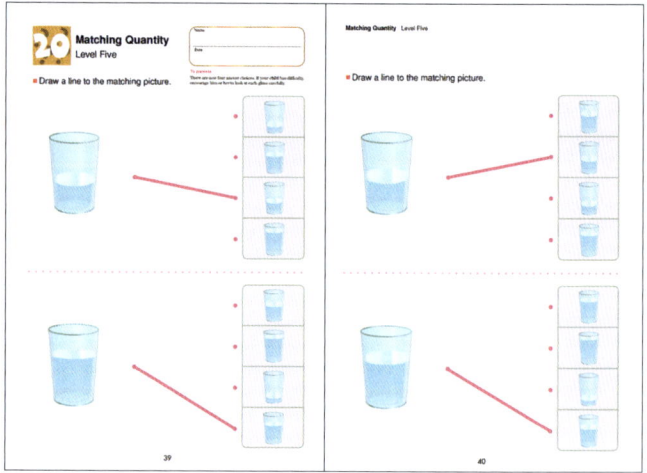

pages 39 and 40

pages 41 and 42

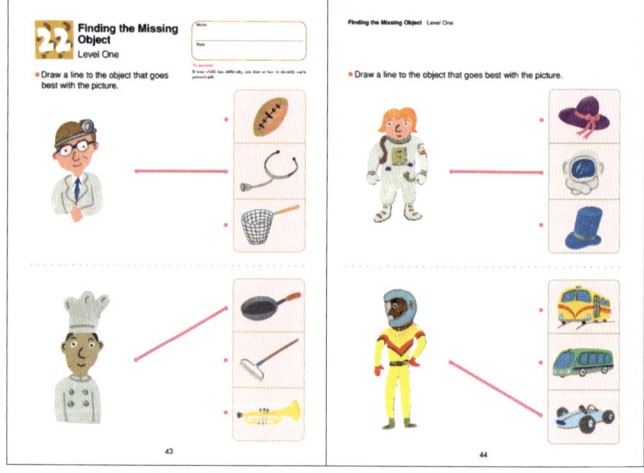

pages 43 and 44

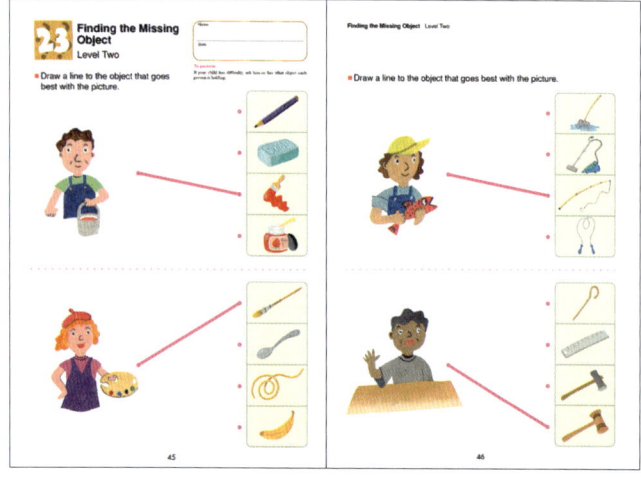

pages 45 and 46

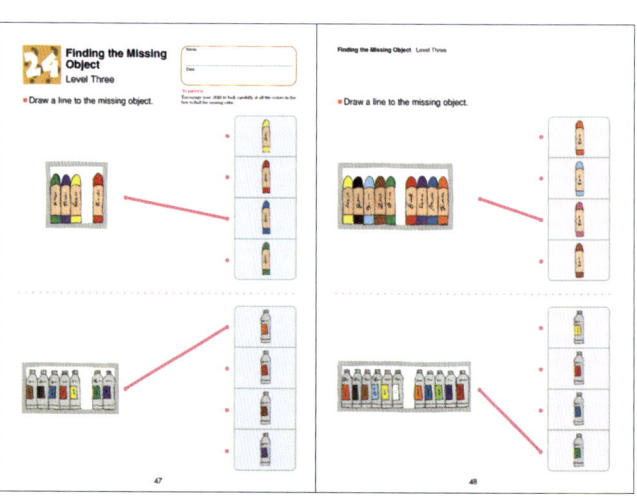

pages 47 and 48

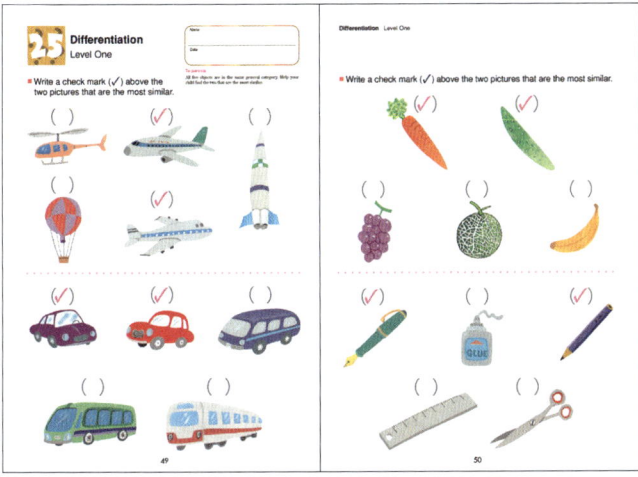

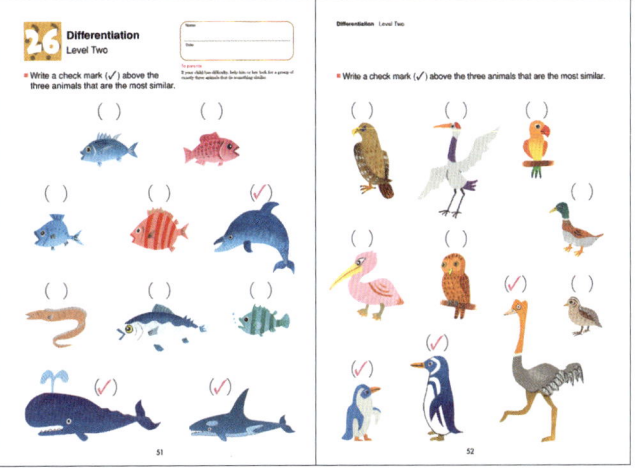

pages 49 and 50

pages 51 and 52

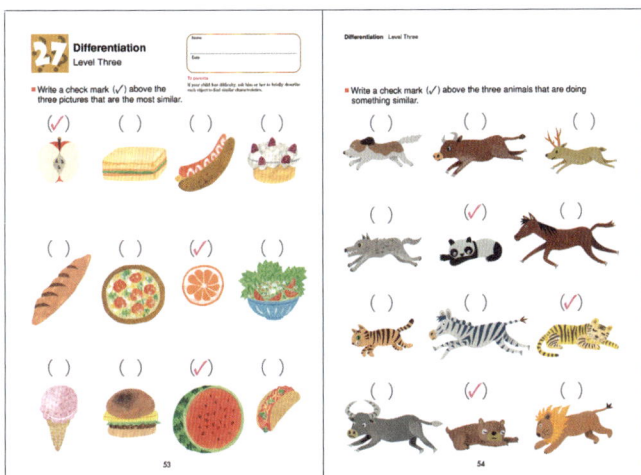
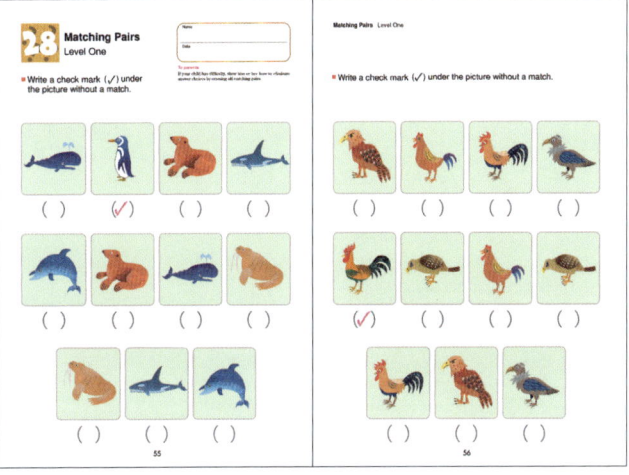

pages 53 and 54

pages 55 and 56

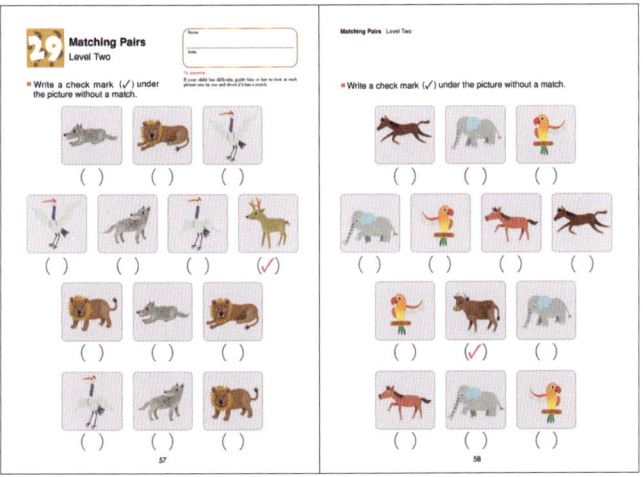
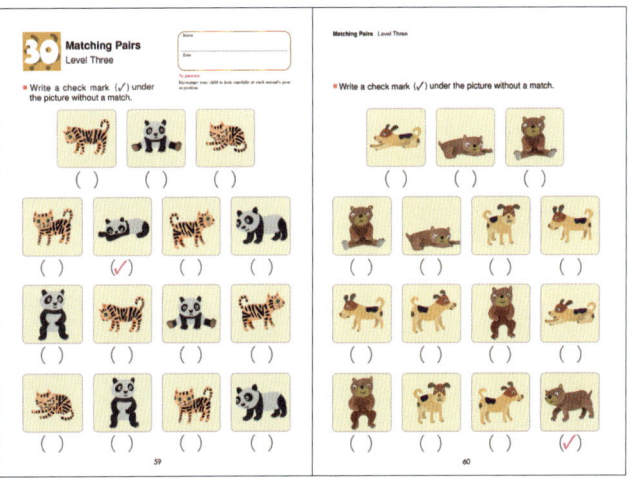

pages 57 and 58

pages 59 and 60

pages 61 and 62

pages 63 and 64

pages 65 and 66

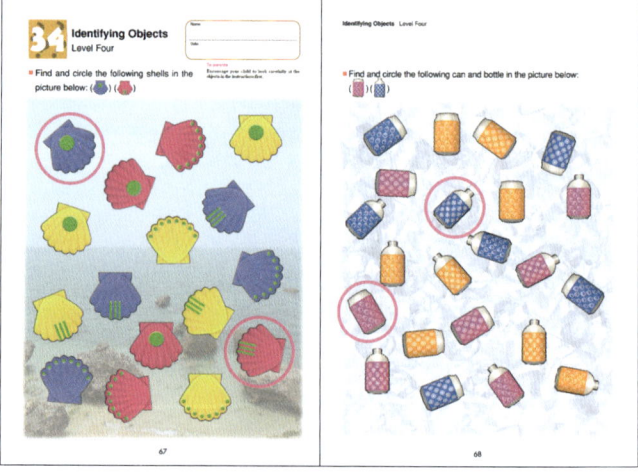

pages 67 and 68

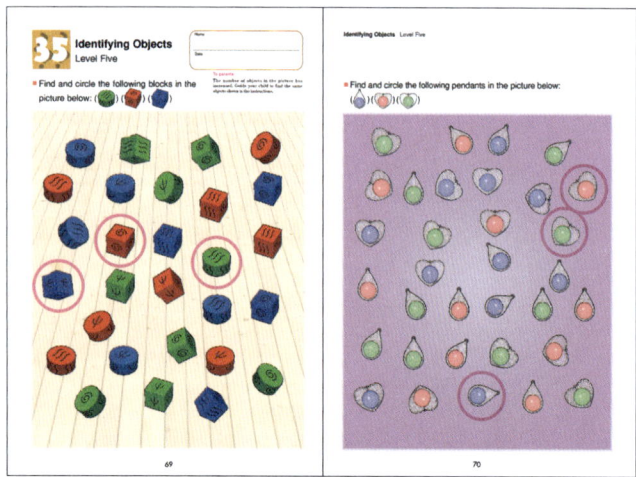

pages 69 and 70

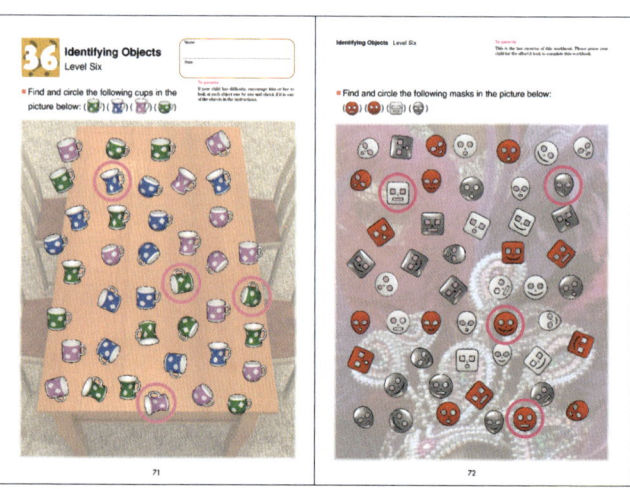

pages 71 and 72

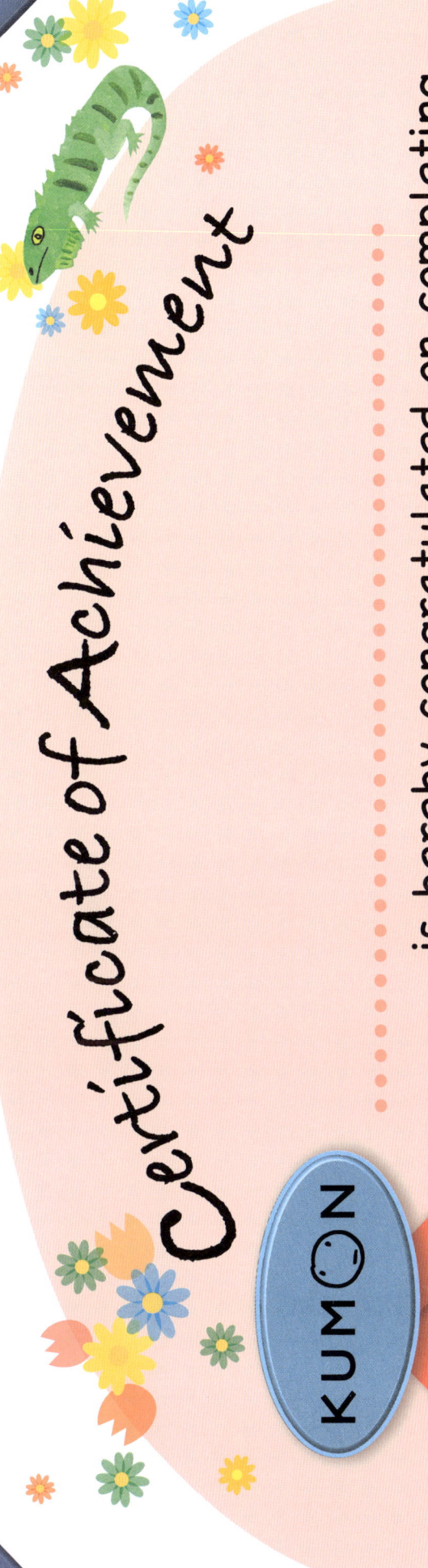

Certificate of Achievement

is hereby congratulated on completing

Thinking Skills Workbooks
Kindergarten Same and Different

Presented on _____ , 20 ____

_____
Parent or Guardian

KUM☺N